Autonomy

and

Foreign Language Learning

Prepared for the

COUNCIL OF EUROPE

by

HENRI HOLEC

Centre de Recherches et d'Applications
Pédagogiques en Langues, Nancy

Published for and on behalf of the

COUNCIL OF EUROPE

by

PERGAMON PRESS

OXFORD · NEW YORK · TORONTO · SYDNEY · PARIS · FRANKFURT

U.K.	Pergamon Press Ltd., Headington Hill Hall. Oxford OX3 0BW, England
U.S.A.	Pergamon Press Inc., Maxwell House, Fairview Park, Elmsford, New York 10523, U.S.A.
CANADA	Pergamon Press Canada Ltd, Suite 104, 150 Consumers Road, Willowdale, Ontario M2J 1P9, Canada
AUSTRALIA	Pergamon Press (Aust.) Pty. Ltd., P.O. Box 544, Potts Point, N.S.W. 2011, Australia
FRANCE	Pergamon Press SARL, 24 rue des Ecoles, 75240 Paris, Cedex 05, France
FEDERAL REPUBLIC OF GERMANY	Pergamon Press GmbH, 6242 Kronberg-Taunus, Hammerweg 6, Federal Republic of Germany

First edition 1979

This Pergamon Press edition 1981

British Library Cataloguing in Publication Data
Holec, Henri
Autonomy and foreign language learning.
1. Language and languages — Study and teaching
2. Independent study
I. Title II. Council of Europe
407   P53   80–41849

ISBN 0–08–025357–1

Printed in Great Britain by A. Wheaton & Co. Ltd., Exeter

PERGAMON INSTITUTE OF ENGLISH (OXFORD)

Council of Europe Modern Languages Project

Autonomy

and

Foreign Language Learning

Other titles in the series

OSKARSSON, M
Approaches to self-assessment in foreign language learning

RICHTERICH, R, and J-L CHANCEREL
Identifying the needs of adults learning a foreign language

TRIM, J L M
Developing a unit/credit scheme of adult language learning

TRIM, J L M, R RICHTERICH, J A VAN EK, and D A WILKINS
Systems development in adult language learning

VAN EK, J A and L G ALEXANDER
Threshold level English

VAN EK, J A, L G ALEXANDER and M A FITZPATRICK
Waystage English

See also
SYSTEM: The International Journal of Educational Technology and Language
Learning Systems. (Free specimen copies available on request.)

The Council of Europe was established by ten nations on 5 May 1949, since when its membership has progressively increased to twenty-one. Its aim is "to achieve a greater unity between its Members for the purpose of safeguarding and realizing the ideals and principles which are their common heritage and facilitating their economic and social progress". This aim is pursued by discussion of questions of common concern and by agreements and common action in economic, social, cultural, scientific, legal and administrative matters.

The Council for Cultural Cooperation was set up by the Committee of Ministers of the Council of Europe on 1 January 1962 to draw up proposals for the cultural policy of the Council of Europe, to coordinate and give effect to the overall cultural programme of the organization and to allocate the resources of the Cultural Fund. All the member governments of the Council of Europe, together with the Holy See and Finland which have acceded to the European Cultural Convention, are represented on the Council for Cultural Cooperation.

The aim of the work carried out by the Council for Cultural Cooperation in the area of modern language learning is to encourage the development of understanding, cooperation and mobility among Europeans by improving and broadening the learning of modern languages by all sections of the population. This aim will be pursued
— by making generally available the basic tools for the systematic planning, construction and conduct of learning programmes geared to the needs and motivations of the learners and to the changing requirements of society;
— by helping to prepare teachers to play their proper roles in such programmes,
— and by further developing a framework for close and effective international cooperation in the promotion of language learning.

For this purpose, and under the authority of the Council for Cultural Cooperation, a number of studies have been prepared, some of which are being published in this Council of Europe Modern Language Series. However, the opinions expressed in the studies written in this framework are not to be regarded as reflecting the policy of any government, of the Committee of Ministers of the Secretary General of the Council of Europe.

Applications for reproduction and translation should be addressed to the Director of Education, Culture and Sport, Council of Europe, Strasbourg (France).

CONTENTS

INTRODUCTION 1

I.   AUTONOMY 3
   1. Definition 3
   2. Useful distinctions 4
   3. Conclusions 7

II. AUTONOMY AND SELF-DIRECTED LEARNINGS OF
     LANGUAGES 9
   1. Fixing of objectives 9
   2. Definition of the contents and progressions 12
   3. Selection of methods and techniques 14
   4. Monitoring of the acquisition procedure 15
   5. Evaluation of what has been acquired 16
   6. Conclusions 19

III. IMPLICATIONS OF SELF-DIRECTED LEARNING...... 21
   1. The new role of the learner 21
   2. New objectives of teaching 23
   3. The teachers' new roles 24
   4. Conclusions: structural consequences 25

IV. EXPERIMENTS 27
   1. The Stirling experiment (Great Britain) 27
   2. The Bournemouth Eurocentre experiment (Great Britain) .. 28
   3. The Study Circles experiment in Sweden 29
   4. Experiments at the Centre de Recherches et d'Applications
       Pédagogiques en Langues (Nancy, France) 30
   5. Conclusions: future developments 32

V.   GENERAL CONCLUSIONS 34

APPENDIX I: Self-directed learning in English as a foreign language —
               Aims and objectives. Questionnaire 35

APPENDIX II: Models for the self-assessment of oral communicative
               skills and their functions 45

SELECTIVE BIBLIOGRAPHY 50

NOTES 53

                                                                              v

INTRODUCTION

The end of the 1960s saw the development in all so-called industrially advanced Western countries of a socio-political tendency characterized by a definition of social progress, no longer in terms of increasing material well-being through an increase in consumer goods and services, but in terms of an improvement in the 'quality of life' — an expression that did not become a slogan until some years later — based on the development of a respect for the individual in society.

This (irreversible) current, has become even more pronounced in recent years and has given rise to various kinds of social awareness, ranging from ecology to the status of women. By reason of its function within the social structure, adult education has very quickly found itself involved in this movement. In the words of P Dominicé:

> "The ideal of a life dependent on factors other than the status or financial satisfactions of a particular occupation is a huge educational venture and calls for an overhaul of scholastic aims in the minds of all concerned".[1]

Thus it comes about that very many of the discussions on educational innovations that have taken place in the sphere of adult education since the beginning of the 1970s have taken into account this new dimension, which was changing their socio-political context, and have concentrated on the part that education could and should play in calling into question once more the relationships between the individual and society.

Despite their wide diversity,[2] the innovatory proposals relating to adult education policy which emerged from these discussions all have one thing in common; they insist on the need to develop the individual's freedom by developing those abilities which will enable him to act more responsibly in running the affairs of the society in which he lives:

> (adult education) . . . "becomes an instrument for arousing an increasing sense of awareness and liberation in man, and, in some cases, an instrument for changing the environment itself. From the idea of man 'product of his society', one moves to the idea of man 'producer of his society'."[3]

Such a tendency could not be imagined without upsetting the structure of adult education and in particular without redefining the place and role in that structure of the person being educated. Thus the concept of 'autonomy' has been born and has developed:

> ". . . the exercise of responsibilities should be made possible and the capacity to assume responsibility and autonomy should be developed . . ."[4]

> "Adult education could contribute towards the improvement of the quality of life by realising the following objectives: equality of opportunity, responsible autonomy, personal fulfilment, democratization of education".[5]

Several European countries have decided to put this new educational concept into practice either by introducing new structures experimentally or by changing already

---

[1] Dominicé, P (1973) *Continuing education for adults in the context of permanent education. Report* CCC/EES (73) 35.

[2] *Cf* in this connection the proposals made by I Illich and P Freire, as well as those which led to the definition of legislation on continuing education in various European countries, etc.

[3] Janne, H (1977) *Organization, content and methods of adult education. Report* CCC/EES (77) 3.

[4] This is one of the three basic principles of permanent education policy laid down by the Steering Group on Permanent Education set up in 1972 by the Council of Europe's Council for Cultural Cooperation. *Cf* Schwartz, B (1977) *Permanent education. Final report* CCC/EP (77) 8 revised.

[5] Janne, H, *op cit.*

existing structures.[6] But, as might have been expected, the qualitative difference separating directed teaching from self-directed learning is so great that none of these first experiments was able satisfactorily to meet this new demand on the part of adult education.[7] But the demand persists and action-research is being continued, especially at the level of certain more limited sectors of adult education such as language training.

The present study has been conceived in this global education context; whose broad outlines we have just sketched out by briefly recalling the changes in adult education principles that have taken place during the past ten years. Its aim is to present a theoretical and practical description of the application of the concept of autonomy in the matter of language learning by adults by showing, in particular, what is meant by self-directed language learning, what implications such a type of learning has for the part played by the learners, teachers and teaching methods and what types of learning structures have been and might be devised for the purpose of introducing such a method of learning.

NB The intention was that the level of generality of this study should be situated:
— neither too high, in order to describe with sufficient detail both the approach to autonomy and its immediate pedagogical implications, thus avoiding limiting the study to major basic principles;
— nor too restricted, in order to present some considerations that can be applied to the greatest possible number of different pedagogical situations, thus avoiding limiting the reader to the specific description of one or another particular example.

---

[6] The reader will find descriptions of most of these innovations in documents produced by the Council of Europe, especially CCC/EES (76) 29 *Trends towards self-management of adult education, six case studies* and CCC/EES (76) 28 *Developments in adult educational structures, five national studies.*

[7] With regard to the development of the concept of autonomy in secondary education, *cf* especially Marbeau, MV (1977) *Autonomous work by pupils* CCC/EGT (77) 15–E.

I. AUTONOMY

The semi-anarchical use of the term 'autonomy' in the different circles concerned with adult education (adults themselves, teachers, planners, research workers, those in charge of training at vocational levels, etc) and the multiplicity of concepts to be found in an area intersecting with that of autonomy[1] obliges us to start by defining what we understand by 'autonomy' in this study.

1. Definition

1.1. According to the definition given by B Schwartz in *L'éducation demain*[2] 'autonomy' is "the ability to assume responsibility for one's own affairs". In the context with which we are dealing, the learning of languages, autonomy is consequently the *ability to take charge of one's own learning.*

1.2. This ability is not inborn but must be acquired either by 'natural' means or (as most often happens) by formal learning, ie in a systematic, deliberate way.

1.3. It is indeed an *ability*, "a power or capacity to do something"[3] and not a type of conduct, "behaviour"[3]. 'Autonomy' is thus a term describing a potential capacity to act in a given situation — in our case, learning — and not the actual behaviour of an individual in that situation.[4]

To say of a learner that he is autonomous is therefore to say that he is capable of taking charge of his own learning and nothing more: all the practical decisions he is going to make regarding his learning can be related to this capacity he possesses but must be distinguished from it (see note below).

1.4. *To take charge of one's learning* is to have, and to hold, the responsibility for all the decisions concerning all aspects of this learning,[5] ie:
— determining the objectives;
— defining the contents and progressions;
— selecting methods and techniques to be used;
— monitoring the procedure of acquisition properly speaking (rhythm, time, place, etc);
— evaluating what has been acquired.

The autonomous learner is himself capable of making all these decisions concerning the learning with which he is or wishes to be involved.

---

[1] cf the discussion of the terms 'self-management', 'autogestion', 'self-learning' and 'participation' presented by Janne, H, *op cit* in the paragraphs devoted to "Trends towards the self-management of adult education".

[2] Schwartz, B (1977) *L'éducation demain* Aubier Montaigne, Paris.

[3] Definitions taken from the *Concise Oxford Dictionary*.

[4] 'Autonomy' is thus different from 'autodidaxy', this latter expression describing a set of behaviours.

[5] The list of the components of learning suggested by us here is intended to specify the areas of application of the decisions to be made. It is a combination of the list given by Dieuzeide, H (cf 'Technologie éducative II: l'école de demain' in *L'éducation* 91, 1971) and that suggested by Janne, H (*op cit*, p 23).

1.5.   Learning taken charge of in this way by the learner is *self-directed* or undertaken *on an autonomous basis*.[6] This acceptance of responsibility for the learning may be done with or without the help of a teacher, with or without the use of teaching aids. We can therefore distinguish self-directed learning with support from 'unorganized' self-directed learning.

Note: Although 'self-directed learning' implies an 'autonomous learner', the latter does not necessarily involve 'self-directed learning'. In other words a learner may have the ability to take charge of his learning without necessarily utilizing this ability to the full when he decides to learn. Different degrees of self-direction in learning may result either from different degrees of autonomy or from different degrees of exercise of autonomy.

1.6.   Learning may be either entirely or only partially self-directed. In order to show the various degrees of self-direction as applied to learning in a concrete form in terms of their physical reality, we reproduce below a table prepared by L Dickinson.[7]

2.   Useful distinctions

2.1. Self-directed learning and distance teaching, programmed teaching etc.

Various kinds of teaching developed over the past 30 years,[8] such as distance teaching (television teaching) and programmed teaching, and the 'learning packages' of all types available in large numbers on the market, all share the common feature of not requiring the presence of a teacher. It has often been concluded from this that the learning which they offer is self-directed learning.

Examining them closely we find that these types of teaching do no more, under the most favourable circumstances, than enable the learner to take charge of the practical organization of his learning (rhythm, time and place) whereas the aims, content, methods and evaluation of that learning are invariably decided from outside, leaving the learner no opportunity to intervene. His responsibility is thus severely restricted and the degree of self-directed learning scarcely justifies the mention of autonomy in such an instance.

In a general way the extent to which a teacher is physically present is not a good standard by which to judge the extent to which learning is self-directed: whether a teacher is present or not as learning proceeds, it is principally the role of the learner which is the determining factor of self-directed learning.

[6] The adjective 'autonomous' can be applied only to a person and not to a process. In the frequently used expression 'autonomous learning', 'autonomous' necessarily assumes a different meaning. To obviate any ambiguity it is preferable to replace this expression by 'self-directed learning'. The expression 'apprentissage en autonomie' ('learning on an autonomous basis') which we also use lacks clarity but has the advantage of forming a bridge between old and new terminology.

[7] Dickinson, L (1978) 'Autonomy, self-directed learning and individualization' in *Self-directed learning and autonomy*, Cambridge, 13–15 December 1976, University of Cambridge, Department of Linguistics. (It should be noted that in this article L Dickinson uses the term autonomy to describe entirely self-directed learning.)

[8] For a discussion of some of these teaching methods cf Henner-Stanchina, C (1976) *Autonomy: A viable strategy for adult language learners* Degree thesis, Nancy University II.

4

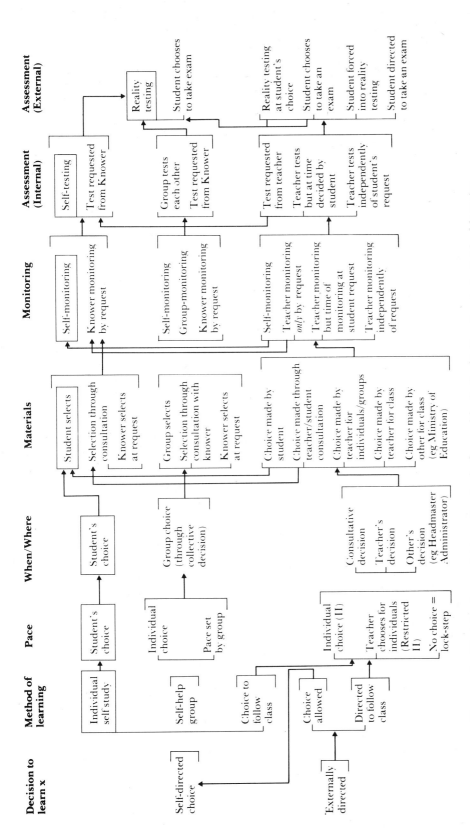

Diagram 1. Sketch of a model to estimate degree and loci of self-direction in individual learning.

2.2. Self-directed learning and individualized teaching

The terms 'individualized teaching' or 'individualization of teaching' or 'individualization of learning' cover a wide variety of different practices.

> "Individualization has been applied to programmes varying from the "traditional 'lock-step' operation" with added individual or small group help, to correspondence courses and totally independent study".[9]

The common feature of all these practices is a desire to increase the degree of adequacy of the teaching for the recipient, the learner. Although derived from a different trend, based in part on work on the psychology of the individual carried out around the start of the century, a trend towards 're-personalization' of the individual which goes far beyond the framework of education (cf the advertising slogans 'long-term personalized credit', 'personalize your home', etc), individualization is similar to autonomy in that it largely takes into account the specific nature of each learner. But there the similarity ends: the educational attitude that inspires individualization, the role assigned to knowledge and the teaching of knowledge on which it is founded and above all the role which it assigns to the learner make it a process very different, if not altogether different, from the process that leads to the autonomization of learning.

> "The attempt to make education more learner-centred has had the effect of encouraging individualization on one hand and autonomy on the other. It is necessary to distinguish carefully between these closely related but distinct concepts. It is possible to pursue individualization in a thoroughly authoritarian framework."[10]

As a matter of fact, in the minds of most of its advocates individualization remains a 'method' of teaching and gives rise to the elaboration and adoption of teaching procedures and not learning procedures.

In a general way the extent to which the learner is taken into consideration forms no criterion for judging the extent to which learning is self-directed: individualization effected by taking into account the learner's needs, his favourite methods of learning, his level, and so on, leave the learner in the traditional position of dependency and do not allow him to control his learning for himself.

> "Every one of the (individualization) schemes mentioned manages to safeguard the nature of the traditional teacher–student hierarchical relationship, students remaining recipients of the material fed into them, whether it be directly or through a machine, by the teacher-specialist."[11]

> "The teacher looks at individuals' problems, but decides himself how different kinds of individual should be treated."[12]

2.3. Self-directed learning and participation

Attempts have been made to develop, over the last ten years, both in the broad socio-political sphere and in that of education, the concept and practice of participation in decision-making, which shares some features of both the trend of 're-personalization' of the individual and that of rendering the individual capable of assuming responsibility. The principle of participation is that of sharing power between those at

---

[9] Dickinson, L, op cit, cf also Logan, G E (1970) 'Curricula for individualization instruction' in Britannica Review of Foreign Language Education, Vol II.

[10] Trim, J L M (1978) 'Some possibilities and limitations of learner autonomy' in Self-directed learning and autonomy, Cambridge, 13–15 December 1976. University of Cambridge, Department of Linguistics.

[11] Henner-Stanchina, C, op cit.

[12] Trim, J L M, op cit.

the 'base' and those at the 'summit' of a decision structure. Such sharing may be of two kinds, involving either allocation of the areas of decision and therefore full responsibility for the decision-maker in his alloted sphere, or proportional allocation of the decision-makers of the base and the summit to each of the areas of decision.

In the field of learning both these types of sharing are found.

However, applications of the first type which would make it possible for learning to be partly self-directed have not really altered the structure of power, the teacher invariably reserving to himself the most important areas of decision (eg the fixing of objectives and evaluation).

As for applications of the second type, these are regularly found to be incapable of encouraging real self-direction of learning:[13] in the most favourable circumstances acceptance of responsibility on the part of both teacher and learner represents in theory, but not in fact, an acceptance of joint responsibility but the institutional structure in which the decisions are made remains unaltered; in the most unfavourable circumstances participation by the learner is merely apparent (and may even act as a safeguard for the maintenance of the 'traditional' situation) and the teacher retains full control over the learning.

3. Conclusions

As shown by this clarification of the concepts of autonomy and self-directed learning — a clarification called for owing to the many semantic distortions to which these terms are subjected in the current phraseology of educators — autonomization of learning implies that the two undermentioned conditions must be satisfied:

— firstly, the learner must have the ability to take charge of his learning, ie he must *know how* to make the decisions which this involves;

— secondly, there must be a learning structure in which control over the learning can be exercised by the learner, ie in which the learner *has the possibility* of exercising his ability to take charge.[14]

The first condition occupies a position logically antecedent to that of the second. But what is the situation in practice when the learner is not autonomous, as is generally the case?

Is it reasonable to hope that an adult learner will be willing to devote time and energy to learning to learn before finding himself a place in the learning structure that will enable him to acquire the knowledge he seeks? And even if this were so, is it possible to learn to learn without learning anything?

[13] cf Dalin, Å (1975) *Towards self-management of learning processes?* CCC/EES (75) 9. There is also a well-known French saying meaning 'Participation is a trap for idiots'.

[14] A third condition might be said to be that the learner should *want* to take charge of his learning. For practical reasons we prefer to regard this desire to take charge as part of the ability to do so: in an actual learning context, desire cannot be put into effect without ability and experience shows that ability cannot be acquired without desire.

The real educational problem involved in the first instance is therefore that of introducing learning systems which will allow both for the acquisition of autonomy and for self-directed learning.

In the second part of this study we propose to look at the implications of the concepts of autonomy and self-directed learning when applied to the sphere of the acquisition of languages, so as to define the problem more accurately before suggesting means of solving it.

II. AUTONOMY AND SELF-DIRECTED LEARNING OF LANGUAGES

A simple way of describing the ability to take charge of language learning is to describe the practical modalities of decision-making which such ability renders possible.

Let us remind ourselves that, with total self-direction, action by the learner is concerned with:

— fixing the objectives
— defining the contents and progressions
— selecting the methods and techniques to be used
— monitoring the acquisition procedure
— evaluating what has been acquired.

Note: We are keeping this subdivision of the learning process but this does not mean that decisions at each of these levels can be made independently of decisions concerning the rest:

"... components (of the education system) such as analysis of needs and evaluation of results must all be considered together and uninterruptedly throughout the entire process".[1]

1. Fixing of objectives

1.1.   Traditionally, ie in directed learning:

1.1.1.   The learning objectives are fixed by the teaching establishment or the teacher.

1.1.2.   This is done:

—through an analysis of the field in which the learning takes place: analysis of the linguistic code in the case of teaching linguistic competence and of verbal communication in the case of teaching communicative competence;

—through an 'objective' analysis of the civilization (in the broad sense) of the country of the target language, when the learning objective includes a 'cultural' dimension;

—lastly, if account is taken of the audience, through the learner's needs and motivations.

1.1.3.   The teaching establishment and teacher define these objectives on the basis of what they regard as the knowledge indispensable to the learner, taking the native speaker as a standard.

1.1.4.   The objectives so determined:
— are fixed once and for all in the temporal framework of the learning (for a year, term, intensive session, etc);
— apply to all learners, usually a group;

[1] Janne, H, *op cit*, p 23.

— are, where necessary, subdivided into intermediate objectives so as to fit in with the teaching structure (objectives for each year in the case of a syllabus covering more than a year) or to conform to the learners' standards on admission, or else for both these reasons; we thus arrive at the 'pilgrim's progress' described by John Trim, adviser to the Modern Languages Project of the Council for Cultural Cooperation.[2]

1.2. In self-directed learning the learner himself defines his objectives and the essential consequence of this will be the introduction of the learner's *specific personal dimension*.[3]

1.2.1. Definition of the objectives will be based on an analysis made by the learner of the final behaviour aimed at, in accordance with his *subjective* criteria.

1.2.1.1.a As regards the communicative competence[4] the learner will take as objective not the verbal behaviour of the abstraction called 'native speaker' but that which he conceives as being his own in the communicative situations in which he will find himself. This will then be integrated behaviour (ie dissociated neither from the situation nor, above all, from the learner himself) described, for example, with the help of statements of the type:
— "I must be capable of doing this in conversation with such and such a speaker, in such and such a sphere . . ."
— "If the person I am speaking to does this I must be capable of reacting in such and such a way . . ."

— "I must be capable of doing (a) and (b) in such and such a manner (cordial/reserved, amusing/serious, formal/informal, quickly/speed being of no consequence, my pronunciation must be perfect/my pronunciation will be of no consequence so long as I am understood, and so on)."

It is thus not only at the level of the *choice* of the communicative acts that the individual character of the learning will appear but also (and it is essentially here that the definition of objectives will show the greatest difference from determination by the teacher or teaching establishment) at the level of the *ways* in which the acts are realized: for a learner who envisages himself as a future speaker the dimensions 'attitude towards the other person', 'personal involvement', 'image of oneself', etc, all of them expressed by verbal behaviour, are naturally an integral part of communication. That which objectively viewed may be considered as a 'variant' may for the learner be the personal norm that he desires to reach :[5] it is in effect (the equivalent as regards communication) language-behaviour which he wishes to make his own, an 'idiolect', and not a language-system.

---

[2] *cf* Trim, J L M (1980) *Developing a unit/credit scheme of adult language learning* Pergamon, Oxford.

[3] In order to make the statement clear and simple the remarks we shall suggest will be *generalizations:* they will be valid for the general body of learners without necessarily being so for each individual one.

[4] An adult is never interested in linguistic competence alone.

[5] In this sense an analysis of the needs on which the learner bases the fixing of his learning objectives brings into play a number of parameters not included in the analyses of 'external' needs which could moreover be included only after preparing a personality description scale.

1.2.1.1.b   On the other hand, as regards the attainment threshold laid down by the learner for each of his objectives, the personal dimension will once again play its part: he himself will decide what is indispensable, what is secondary and what is useless. As a result the attainment threshold aimed at will vary according to the learner's 'temperament' and there will be a wide gap between the threshold of the 'perfectionist' and that of the 'laxist'.[6]

1.2.1.2.   In the same way as regards the cultural dimension of his learning only some aspects of the foreign civilization will be of real interest to him, namely those that will enable him to build up his own view of the civilization in question.

1.2.2.   The objectives and learning thresholds will not necessarily be fixed for all time; the learner may look at them again as his learning continues and alter them.

Any possible alterations, whether partial or total, may be the result of various factors.

1.2.2.1.   *Changes occurring in the external situation forming the learning environment:*

— professional or vocational situation: where the motive for learning is professional or vocational, any change in language needs connected with such occupation will involve a change of objective (eg a change in the function of communication in a foreign language as part of the work contemplated or a change in the work as a whole, and so on);
— social situation: where the motive for learning is a social one, certain changes in this field may involve a change of objective (eg where the learner wishes to be able to communicate among a circle of acquaintances, the addition of new individuals speaking a different dialect, etc);
— material situation: changes of all kinds may involve a change of objective (eg a move to another area making it possible to receive foreign television, etc).

1.2.2.2.   *Changes occurring in the internal learning situation:*

— level of knowledge: as his level of knowledge of the language he is learning changes the learner may be led to amend his initial objectives either because some objectives regarded as unattainable become attainable or on the other hand because objectives regarded as attainable prove unattainable or because fresh objectives are revealed in the light of knowledge already acquired; thus in fact developments in any learning experience may be the reason for a change in objectives;
— finally it must not be forgotten that the learner may simply change his mind.

---

[6] A learner fixing his threshold at a level which would not allow him to communicate (a currently widespread fear among language teachers) would simply reveal:
   — either that he has not known how to make a proper evaluation (*cf* II–5: Evaluation) if he makes his assessment at the end of the course: or
   — that mastery of a communicative competency is not his main purpose.

1.3. Conclusions[7]

1.3.1.   As regards the definition of objectives therefore, self-direction of learning entails some very big differences as compared with definition made from outside by a teacher or teaching establishment. To sum up, the 'pilgrim's progress' towards an objective based essentially on the field of learning, the same for everyone, is replaced by progressive steps (a succession of objectives) of a diverse nature fixed for and by each learner by reference to his personal needs and motivations, progressive steps which may be challenged and amended by the learner at any time.

1.3.2.   To be autonomous is to be capable of dealing with the definition of objectives of this kind.

2.   Definition of the contents and progressions

The contents and progressions form the materials—and their sequential organization — which enable the objectives to be realized. Definition of them is closely linked with the definition of objectives and, indeed, it sometimes happens that one of them is defined in terms of the other.

2.1.   In directed learning the contents and progressions are defined by the teachers who 'have the knowledge'.

2.1.1.   The contents are defined in terms of lexis, grammar and phonology:
— as regards lexis the choice is usually made on the basis of frequency lists, possibly supplemented by a 'specialized vocabulary';

— as regards grammar the principle is approximately the same: basic structures and possibly distinct structures (stylistic dimension);

— as regards phonology, since the elements available for selection are somewhat limited in number the whole is generally made an integral part of the curriculum: pronunciation of phonemes, intonation, rhythm.

For all three components a single norm (dialect, register, level) is adopted, perhaps with a few limited incursions into other norms.

2.1.2.   In a general way the approach is 'globalistic', ie the contents are regarded as necessary for the learning of both comprehension and expression, sometimes even for both oral and written learning (this is essentially owing to the fact that methods of learning different skills are not generally differentiated one from another).

2.1.3.   With regard to progressions, these are based on the degree of 'profitability' of the elements incorporated as judged by frequency and on the degree of their complexity. The progressions are generally rather slow and result in learning being spread out over a rather long period.

2.2.   In self-directed learning the contents will as a general rule be defined by the learner, both in a more restrictive manner, to the extent that only those

[7] This section devoted to objectives should be closely related to that covering evaluation, since the objectives must be determined so as to be capable of evaluation, and since evaluation cannot be done except in relation to objectives. Some of the problems that may arise in this section will therefore find answers in the chapter on evaluation.

12

verbal elements necessary for realizing the selected communicative functions (cf objectives) are incorporated into the curriculum, and more widely, to the extent that mastery of the personal dimension of communication will require a number of additional verbal and non-verbal elements.

2.2.1. One of the two fundamental features of definition of contents by the learner is that the thematic content of the communication aimed at is given priority. The learner wants above all to communicate (to understand and to express) significations and the choice of forms is made only secondarily by reference to significations. Thus the contents will be defined only secondarily in terms of lexis, grammar and phonology. The process will actually be as follows (expressed in terms of propositions which the learner will possibly be called upon to construct):

— which are the 'ideas' I wish to understand and which are the 'ideas' I wish to express?[8]
— which are the words and grammar I must master so as to understand the first and express the second?

As regards the choice of norm, this will be made in a much more flexible and more appropriate manner: it will be made on the basis of communicative situations (defined particularly by reference to the others involved in the conversations and the thematic content) and on the proposed method of communication (comprehension and/or expression).

Note: The thematic contents are of course determined on the basis of personal choices and not on the basis of the choices of the majority of the class-group or the subjective choices of the teacher.

2.2.2. The second fundamental feature of the definition of contents by the learner is that those contents are no longer 'brought in' from outside but are to some extent 'created' by the learner. He will have to discover those contents by observing and analysing the sources of information available to him:[9] written texts, sound recordings, video recordings, films, dictionaries, grammars, etc. These sources will also include both educational and authentic documents, and native speakers.[10]

2.2.3. As for progressions, these are determined not by reference to the linguistic content but on the basis of communicative and thematic priorities fixed by the learner for himself. As a rule they will be fairly rapid, since an adult learner is hardly ever in a position to spread his learning over a very long period of time.

---

[8] The two sets of 'ideas' may overlap, but not necessarily so (I may want to understand what my doctor tells me but the things I have to tell him may be quite different).

[9] Every discovery is a creation for the person making it even if the thing discovered was already known to others.

[10] Experience shows that this discovery is simpler than would appear since the learner has at his disposal the valuable tool consisting of the communicative and linguistic intuition acquired in his mother tongue. Moreover it becomes easier and easier as his knowledge increases.

2.3. Conclusions

2.3.1.   With regard to the definition of contents, the fundamental originality of acting on an autonomous basis is to be found firstly in the new way of looking at the knowledge to be acquired as presupposed by such definition and secondly in the new learner/knowledge relationship brought into operation (this will be referred to again in Chapter III, *cf* p 25 *et seq*). This means dividing knowledge into *useful knowledge* and *useless knowledge* at each stage of the learning, in a different manner from the 'traditional' division.

2.3.2.   With respect to definition of progressions, acting on an autonomous basis involves abandoning rigid progressions determined by reference to linguistic inventories prepared in a 'scientific' way, since immediate 'profitability' is more important than long-term 'profitability'.

2.3.3.   Being autonomous means being capable of defining the contents and progressions of one's learning in this way.

3.   Selection of methods and techniques

3.1.   Without going back to the various ways in which the choice of methods and techniques is carried out in self-directed learning, we may simply remind ourselves that the selection varies according to the greater or lesser amount of trust placed in one theory of learning or another, to the belief (sometimes amounting to fanaticism) in this or that teaching method, to the importance attached to one technical tool or another, but also according to the lessons drawn from experience, to the educational intuition gained by practice in combination with creative imagination, and so on and so on.

In the present state of knowledge regarding the process of language learning by adults it is a difficult and risky business to work out teaching methods and techniques suitable for the learners and this explains the great diversity of solutions suggested.[11]

3.2.   In self-directed learning the learner himself will be defining his methods and techniques.

3.2.1.   He will not make this definition *a priori* before starting his studies but right at the beginning and as his studies continue. He will in fact proceed by trial and error: by using the methods and techniques he has chosen and then evaluating them he will be able to decide which are appropriate to his own case.

3.2.2.   As a rule this empirical process will not involve any loss of learning time: in the first place the investment thus decided upon at the start of his studies will be to a large extent offset by the improved quality of later learning, besides this the number of trials and errors will never be very great since there is nothing to prevent the learner from thinking the matter over and picking out from all the possible alternatives those that are most likely to be suitable.

[11] The study of this process is only in its infancy *cf* the work done at Kiel University in the Federal Republic of Germany by Wode *et al*, that of Krashen *et al* at the University of Southern California, USA (*see Second language acquisition and second language learning* by Stephen Krashen (1981) Pergamon, Oxford).

3.2.3.   The methods and techniques that will be available to the learner include:

— those that he knows because he has used them in earlier studies (especially language studies);

— those he will learn of from other learners or in miscellaneous teaching materials;

— those he will devise for himself.

3.2.4.   The criteria he will use for selection purposes will be of two kinds:

— criteria of efficacy as regards the objectives set: knowing exactly what his objectives are and making his own assessments of progress made, the learner will be able to determine accurately enough how far the methods and techniques he has used have been effective; this judgment, coupled with what he has learnt during his studies, will enable him to make valid assumptions as to the reasons for the failure of any particular method or technique where he has been let down in any way and to plan his decisions for the next attempt;

— criteria regarding adaptation to external and internal constraints on the learner: the proposed methods and techniques must be adapted as far as possible to constraints of all kinds affecting the learner during his studies — restrictions in the matter of place, time, materials, etc — and must fit in as far as possible with the type of learner that every adult is — restrictions whose characteristics range from his type of memory to qualities such as perseverance, patience, and so on, and to the value attached by the learner to any particular activity.

3.3.   Conclusions

3.3.1.   Definition by the learner himself of the methods and techniques to be used in his studies is far more likely, in the present state of knowledge, to lead to success than is definition of them from outside. In a general way this is what happens when the 'consumer' is also the 'producer'. There is no doubt, however, that if, in the future, research into the acquisition of second languages could make it possible to enlighten and direct the learner's intuition, those chances would be enhanced still further.

3.3.2.   Being autonomous means being capable of selecting one's learning methods and techniques in the way we have just described.

4.   Monitoring the acquisition procedure

4.1   The acquisition procedure has reference to spatial and temporal dimensions: where the acquisition takes place, at what times, according to what timetable, at what rhythm, and so on. Adult audiences are distinctive in that contrary to 'vocational' learners involved in a schools system they are subject to spatial and temporal restrictions that are often very rigid and always very specific to each individual. Among those restrictions it should be in particular noted that very often the end of the course is fixed so far as the learner is concerned, either because he has been 'credited' a certain

15

length of time or because he has to make use of the ability he seeks to acquire at some definite time, determined in advance.

In these circumstances the learning rhythms are all the more varied because the speed of learning, which differs from one learner to another, is complicated by the multiplicity of overall timetables.

In addition the psychological and intellectual availability of adults with their professional and vocational commitments, together with fatigue and preoccupations of all kinds, is extremely irregular and unpredictable: the best time for learning and the length of time devoted to it occur at very different periods in time for different individuals.

4.2.   It is partly in order to cope with this situation that instruction tends towards individualization: distance teaching and programmed instruction, for example, must enable the learner to cope with the spatial and temporal restrictions imposed upon him by his environment and to arrange to do his learning at times most convenient to himself.

However, this is not always possible, especially where the course begins and ends for everyone at the same time, where the mid-term and final examinations are held on the same dates for everyone, and so on.

4.3.   In self-directed learning the student decides for himself when to study, how long to work at a time, and he can therefore adjust his learning rhythm to his acquisition rhythm. Where the end of the course is decided for him by others, he can to some extent overcome this restriction by speeding up his learning rhythm either by devoting more time to his studies or by increasing the number of maximally effective sessions.

5.   Evaluation of what has been acquired

'Evaluation of what has been acquired' may be understood to mean very different operations which need to be distinguished one from another.

5.1.   To begin with *evaluation* must be distinguished from *certification*.

"Evaluation functions and techniques should not be confused with those relating to certification . . . Certification necessitates evaluation, although the converse is not true".[12]

Certification is based on an appraisement of knowledge made by reference to and in order to obtain a certificate. It is an appraisement made outside the learning process and which obeys rules of a sociological nature in relation to which the learner as such has no power to make decisions. The only freedom allowed him is that of choosing whether or not he shall direct his learning towards obtaining a certificate.

In a self-directed system of learning the learner **must** be able to make a choice, which means that certification must not be compulsory:

"Certification should be confined to courses conferring qualifications: it should not be allowed to become the compulsory objective or the required terminus".[13]

[12] Porcher, L (1979) 'The functions of evaluation in a European unit/credit system for modern language learning by adults' in the *Report of the Symposium held at Ludwigshafen-am-Rhein, 7–14 September 1977*. Strasbourg.

[13] Scwartz, B (1977) *Permanent education. Final report* CCC/EP (77) 8 revised.

5.2.　In evaluation, strictly speaking a distinction must be made between *external evaluation* and *internal evaluation*.

5.2.1.　External evaluation is that by which at the end of the studies (when the final objective or the intermediate objectives are deemed to have been achieved) the learner's attainments are appraised by reference to criteria applicable to all the learners which enable his attainments to be assigned a place in relation to the content of the learning and/or the attainments of other learners.

"Its nature (ie the nature of outside evaluation) is such as to favour standardized language teaching and courses. It focuses on the subject matter to be learned . . . The purpose is to measure results (intermediate or final)".[14]

The criteria adopted in making an evaluation of this kind are naturally defined by the teaching establishment or teacher, since the learner cannot use knowledge that he does not possess for the purpose of appraising his attainments.

In such circumstances the amount of responsibility that a learner can have in outside evaluation is extremely limited and superficial: the most he can do is to conduct for himself the tests or other means of evaluation laid down by others and perhaps correct them himself with the help of grids provided for him. Here again the only latitude he can, and should, have is to decide whether or not to submit to this kind of evaluation.

5.2.2.　Internal evaluation is the only kind, strictly speaking, that forms an integral part of the learning in the same way as the definition of objectives, contents, etc, since it is the only kind operating within the learning process, ie which is a constituent part of that process:

". . . an internal part of the learning process without which no learning can be achieved".[15]

It is one of the stages of learning, that during which the learner evaluates the attainments he has lately made as compared with what he was aiming at so that, in the first place, he can be certain that he really has acquired something — and the learning process is not at an end until this evaluation, whether positive or negative, has been carried out — and in the second place so that he can plan his subsequent learning.[16]

It is therefore a type of evaluation whose purpose, unlike that of external evaluation, is not to evaluate the learner's "linguistic ability in terms of his success in mastering course contents"[17] or by reference to the attainments of other learners but to determine to what extent the results achieved are in line with his objective.

It is this crucial evaluation,[18] centred on the learning, for which the learner must assume responsibility in self-directed learning. It is this assumption of responsibility that amounts to real self-evaluation.

[14] Porcher, L, *op cit*.

[15] Henner-Stanchina, C, and Holec, H (1977) 'Evaluation in an autonomous learning scheme' in *Mélanges Pédagogiques* CRAPEL, Nancy.

[16] For further details *cf* Henner-Stanchina, C, and Holec, H, *op cit*.

[17] Porcher, L, *op cit*.

[18] Although there may be learning without certification or external evaluation there cannot be learning without internal evaluation.

5.3. The fundamental characteristic of self-evaluation, as well as of the definition of objectives with which it is very closely bound up, is that it integrates the learner's specific personal dimension.

5.3.1. With regard to criteria used in evaluation, these are chosen by the learner, from all possible criteria, by reference to his own definition of the component parts of successful attainment and the relative importance thereof.

These component parts will perhaps include, for any given learner, the traditional features of correct grammar and lexical wealth, but correct pronunciation will perhaps give way to intelligibility and fluency, and 'variety of style' (making it possible to suit the performance to the mood, atmosphere, etc of the moment) may possibly be regarded as very important or indeed essential.[19] Moreover this choice need not necessarily be final: for each new step in his learning the learner may select other criteria and other combinations of them which are better suited to his new learning objective and in line with his new level of knowledge.

5.3.2. As for the threshold by reference to which his attainments will be regarded as successful or otherwise as determined by each criterion, this will be fixed by the learner according to his own ideas of what is a satisfactory performance.

In addition, this threshold, as determined for each criterion, will not necessarily remain unchanged throughout the whole course since the learner's ideas may change as he considers one performance or another according to the objective aimed at, the level of knowledge gained, etc.

5.3.3. Self-evaluation, ie internal evaluation carried out by the learner, represents a key-level of self-directed learning possibly even to a greater extent than does definition of objectives.

Self-directed learning that did not include acceptance of responsibility for evaluating attainments would not only be incomplete but would run the risk of rapidly becoming directed learning owing to the retroactive effect of the monitoring then exercised by the outside evaluator on the definition of objectives and the fixing of contents.[20]

5.4. This evaluation, regarded from the standpoint of appraisal of linguistic and communicative acquisitions, is supplemented in self-directed learning by evaluation of the learning itself:

"As a language learner, one needs feedback and input information on learning strategies, learning techniques, etc, in other words, on the suitability and effectiveness of learning in relation to personal learning criteria and personal goals. This information will increase the learner's awareness of how he learns and help him make decisions as to the continuation or modification of his learning activities".[21]

This self-evaluation of learning, like that of acquisition, will be carried out on the basis of *personal criteria* such as compatibility between the proposed

[19] For fuller details cf Henner-Stanchina, C, and Holec, H, *op cit.*

[20] A number of suggestions on the exercise of self-evaluation in language are made in Oskarsson, M (1980) *Approaches to self-assessment in foreign language learning*, Pergamon, Oxford, and in Henner-Stanchina, C, and Holec, H, *op cit.*

[21] cf Henner-Stanchina, C, and Holec, H, *op cit.*

18

methods and techniques and the external constraints (availability of place and time; physical possibilities, etc) and internal constraints (intellectual and physical ability, etc) and by reference to *personal thresholds*.[2]

As a general rule it will lead the learner to evaluate how he has taken charge of his learning, from the definition of objectives and contents to selection of methods and techniques, monitoring the learning procedure and evaluating what has been acquired.

6.   Conclusions

6.1.   As we come to the end of this chapter on the characterization of self-directed learning of languages, the aim of which was to indicate and express in practical form what autonomous learning is, we come up against the problem of the interdependence of the decisions made at each stage of the learning process. As we have said, the choices adopted at each of these stages are dependent on those made at other stages. This interdependence, however, operates at different levels: although definition of objectives and evaluation of what has been acquired cannot be imagined one without the other, the relationship between definition of objectives and fixing of contents is not so close, since definition of objectives governs to a very high degree the choice of contents yet does not make that choice imperative; as regards the relationship between contents on the one hand and methods and techniques on the other, although it does in fact exist in that it is not possible for no matter what sort of content to be mastered by any method whatsoever, the relationship does nevertheless come about in an asymmetrical fashion (contents must not be determined by methods, even though in reality this still happens far too often in language teaching) and on the other hand it allows a good deal of latitude for decision (a fair number of methods and techniques make it possible to acquire a given content); finally, monitoring learning procedure appears to have very little connection with the other learning levels.

6.2.   In these circumstances what can one conclude as to the possible degrees of self-direction in learning? Can we conceive of partial and supplementary degrees of acceptance of responsibility on the part of the learner, the teaching establishment or the teacher?

In theory and in practice it is only the level of the monitoring of learning procedure that can be dissociated from the rest: consequently this represents the only possible example of divided responsibility and it is not by chance that this method has come to be used in the less conventional forms of teaching and learning (distance teaching and programmed teaching).

As regards the remaining levels of learning, it is practically impossible to make different parties responsible for these — eg to let the learner assume responsibility or defining objectives and contents whilst the teacher looks after evaluation and the choice of methods and techniques; — indeed the differences in criteria adopted by the various parties would involve a danger

---

[22] For further details *cf* Henner-Stanchina, C, and Holec, H, *op cit.*

19

of imperfect adjustment of the decisions to suit different levels of learning or even that the decisions made by the institutionally stable party (the teacher) would actually dominate those of the institutionally transient party (the learner).

From this standpoint therefore there are no possible degrees of self-direction in learning.

6.3. If we can speak of degrees of self-direction in learning, this can be only in terms of the help which the learner can obtain during the time of his acceptance of responsibility. A learner who is not yet autonomous or not entirely so or is in the process of acquiring autonomy must nevertheless, as we have seen, assume responsibility for the whole of his learning although he may benefit from help given by a teacher or derived from teaching aid (*cf* learning with support). This help, which may be large or small (though without ever amounting to transfer of responsibility) consequently entails an 'alleviation' of the burden of responsibility (the component parts of which we have described in this chapter). In this sense it is then possible to distinguish different degrees of self-direction, determined by the relative proportion of decisions made with or without support.

6.4. The nature and operation of self-directed learning imply, as we have found, redefinition of the learner's role. But they also imply redefinition of the roles of the teacher and the teaching establishment. These are the implications we now propose to examine.

III. IMPLICATIONS OF
SELF-DIRECTED LEARNING

1. The new role of the learner

1.1.   As pointed out by H Janne in his analysis of self-management of education, and this applies *mutatis mutandis* to self-directed language learning, acceptance of responsibility for the learning by the learner involves two fundamental changes in the context of learning: a change in the *definition of the knowledge* to be acquired and a change in the *learner/knowledge* relationship.

> "Self-management of education . . . modifies the relationship between the learner and existing 'knowledge', and on the other hand it modifies the way in which knowledge itself is built up and is developed".[1]

1.1.1.   As regards the knowledge or know-how to be acquired, although this may theoretically be defined globally, ie by considering the totality of the attainments which potentially all learners might adopt as objectives and without prejudging the choice of each of them, and objectively, ie by some party other than the learner and who would describe this knowledge or know-how by analysing the use made of it by a native speaker,[2] it cannot, however, be defined where it has reference to a particular learner. As we have seen, every learner determines his own objectives and contents by making choices based on personal criteria and from all the communication potentialities open to him and this is how he defines the knowledge or know-how he wishes to acquire. In linguistic terms each learner therefore defines the idiolect he wants to master and that idiolect cannot exist apart from him, even if its component elements are part of a language-system shared by the entire community.

Objective, universal knowledge is therefore replaced by subjective, individual knowledge.

1.1.2.   In this way the learner/knowledge relationship is completely upset; the learner is no longer faced with an 'independent' reality that escapes him, to which he cannot but give way, but with a reality which he himself constructs and dominates, even if this cannot be done in an anarchical or uncertain manner.

Note: Let us recall here (*cf* p 13) that such a construction of a reality does not mean that the learner 'invents' a new language; he defines his idiolect by reference to observation and analysis of sources of information derived from various kinds of documents and from informants.

1.2.   In its turn this new learning context changes the learner/learning relationship. The position of passivity and dependence in which the learner was necessarily confined because the knowledge was not accessible to him without the help of an expert-teacher is no longer tenable. Freed from the

---

[1] Janne, H, *op cit*, p 24.

[2] Verbal communication in any language has an advantage over most other learning objectives in that it 'exists' in the objective reality.

need for a mediator actually possessing this knowledge, the learner is *ipso facto* freed from the need for mediatization (instruction): it is no longer essential for the learning to be taken charge of by the teacher, the learner himself can assume responsibility for it.

1.3.   This (potential) acceptance of responsibility, defining the learner's new roles (and which we have described in the previous chapter), can operate only if two conditions are fulfilled: that the learner is willing and that he is also capable of assuming responsibility.

1.3.1.   As regards the first condition it must be emphasized, with B Schwartz, that:

"participation in education in our present day societies must be learnt, does not occur automatically and is not a response to a spontaneous aspiration".[3]

But it should also be noted that this state of things is not irreversible, its cause not being written into the history of the development of mankind.

"Many people feeling a need for education are frightened by the opportunities for participation offered to them and are too inhibited to make use of them. This is the result of their early directive schooling followed by conditioning and alienating occupational activities".[4]

1.3.2.   The same remarks may apply as regards the second condition: few adults are capable of assuming responsibility for their learning, as proved by experience,[5] for the simple reason that they have never had occasion to use this ability. With the majority of them, therefore, autonomy has to be acquired.

In essence this acquisition will bring two different processes into play:

— a gradual *'deconditioning' process* which will cause the learner to break away, if only by putting them into words, from *a priori* judgments and prejudices of all kinds that encumber his ideas about learning languages and the role he can play in it — to free himself from the notion that there is one ideal method, that teachers possess that method, that his knowledge of his mother tongue is of no use to him for learning a second language, that his experience as a learner of other subjects, other know-how, cannot be transferred even partially, that he is incapable of making any valid assessment of his performance, and so on;

— a gradual *process of acquiring* the knowledge and know-how he needs in order to assume responsibility for his learning; to learn to use tools such as dictionaries and grammar books, to assemble and analyse a corpus, to describe his expectations in terms that will serve to define a learning process, all of which implies discovering descriptive categories which will not necessarily be those of a linguist or a professional teacher; to learn to analyse his performance, and so on.

It is through the parallel operation of these two processes that the learner will gradually proceed from a position of dependence to one of independence, from a non-autonomous state to an autonomous one.

1.3.3.   In order for the two conditions essential for actualizing the acceptance of responsibility to be brought together it is necessary, though this is perhaps

---

[3] Schwartz, B, CCC/EP (77) 8 revised, p 15.

[4] Schwartz, B, *ibid*.

[5] Experience also shows that there is no correlation between level of studies and autonomy.

not enough (*cf* Chapter V, *General conclusions*) that a new type of instruction be offered to the learner.

2. New objectives of teaching

2.1.   In a general way teaching coming under the heading of action based on autonomy should no longer be looked upon as *'producing'* learning but as *'facilitating'* it. It must take place in the shape of a set of procedures most of which are still to be discovered, procedures that help the learner to learn and not that make him learn, and which are used by the learner rather than 'mould' him.

Note: This is also fully in accord with the new concepts of foreign language learning derived from current research and according to which learning is not a passive process of stock-piling information supplied by the teaching but, on the contrary, an active, creative operation by means of which the learner converts into acquired knowledge information provided for him in an organized manner (teaching) or in non-organized form ('natural' untreated information).

This new concept of the function of teaching in learning goes very much further than the simple distinction between directive and non-directive teaching.

2.2.   As regards the teaching objectives properly speaking, these are essentially twofold:

— firstly the objective of teaching must be to help the learner acquire the linguistic and communicative abilities he has defined for himself;

— secondly the teaching must also help the learner acquire autonomy for himself, ie to learn to learn.

"To lead the learner from an initially dependent to a finally independent position should be one of the built-in educational objectives of a learning programme".[6]

These two objectives must be pursued together in so far as, in accordance with what we have already said (*cf* p 7), it is out of the question to regard autonomy as a precondition of language learning and since it would be absurd to proceed to learn autonomy when learning of the language is finished.

This raises the problem of how far the methods adopted to achieve the first objective and to achieve the second are compatible. One example will suffice to place this problem in its right perspective: something such as 'programmed instruction' which would perhaps be suitable for helping the learner to acquire a knowledge of a language would nevertheless place him in a position of dependence and irresponsibility such as would immediately conflict with his aim of achieving autonomy.

2.3.   The practical means of organizing and operating such teaching have begun to be investigated in various pilot experiments (*cf* Chapter IV) but there is still much to be done in defining them and putting them into effect in the field of future education.

[6] *cf* Trim, J L M, *op cit.*

3. The teachers' new roles

3.1.　In a system where the learner assumes responsibility for his learning whilst still learning how to do so, where the teaching is centred on giving support to the learner, the teacher himself must also redefine his role by reference to this focusing on the learner and his learning.

Without being in a position to define exhaustively in what way teachers are to intervene in the system (but *cf* Chapter IV on current experiments and *infra*) one may anticipate that the functions of the teacher will in part still be what they sometimes are in a directed system (research into the field of foreign language acquisition, research into the field of language learning methodology, the 'supply' of authentic or organized materials, etc) but will change very considerably in the matter of 'help' and 'advice' which will constitute the support needed by a learner learning to learn at the same time as he acquires a language.[7] The teacher will have to help the learner develop his ability to:

— define his objectives, ie help him to find and use descriptive categories sufficiently 'refined' to enable him to define his learning objectives based on definition of needs; at the very least this means sensibilization to the functioning of verbal communication (by thinking about communicative behaviour in the mother tongue, for example);

— to define contents and progressions to be made, ie to help him assemble learning *corpora* and analyze them in order to extract those linguistic and communicative elements forming the subject to be learnt; at the very least this means supplying information on the possible sources of learning materials (authentic and/or didactic) and preparation for the techniques of describing and classifying linguistic information (composing card-indexes, glossaries etc);

— to choose methods and techniques, ie to help him draw up lists of learning activities and decide what use they are; this will imply developing educational competence based initially on a list of techniques in use (those suggested in different manuals, for example), then observation of his own learning behaviour, and on information regarding language learning processes for adults);

— to monitor the learning procedure, ie essentially to help him realistically to take account of constraints of all kinds that press upon him and to impose a suitable working 'discipline' upon himself;

— to evaluate what he has acquired and his learning process, ie to seek out and use personal appraisal criteria and thresholds based on personal expectations: this will imply the introduction of performance situations (encounters with native speakers, for example) and the elaboration of performance analysis tools and techniques (development of a descriptive linguistic competence, for example).

---

[7] *cf* the suggestions on the role of helper put forward by Henner-Stanchina, C (1976) in *Autonomy: A viable strategy for adult language learners* Degree thesis, University of Nancy II, and those on the tutor made by Scheffknecht, J J (1975) in *The tutor* CCC, Strasbourg.

Concurrently with this the teacher will need to help the learner to appreciate and overcome the 'conditioning' resulting from his previous learning experience which influences his ideas about learning a foreign language.

3.2. As a rule, therefore, in contrast to the apprehension often created by the concept of autonomy in learning, the teacher will find his role becomes more varied rather than curtailed, strengthened rather than weakened (not in terms of authority but in terms of competence) and much greater demands will be made on his creativity than on his highly developed knowledge of teaching techniques. The traditional teacher who might have been regarded as 'replaceable' (cf teaching machines) will give way to a teacher whose role in the process of developing the learner will be irreplaceable. His status will no longer be based on the power conferred by hierarchical authority but on the quality and importance of his relationship to the learner.

3.3. This new definition of the teacher's functions will of course give rise to an acute problem concerning training, particularly in the immediate future, but it will also give rise to others of an institutional nature that are just as practical and urgent:

". . . will there be a high proportion of *full-time* educators, or will there be a majority of experts, counsellors, consultants and assistants, all *part-time?* What qualifications will be required in either case? How much importance will be attached to experience? How will qualifications be awarded and classed? . . ."[8]

These are all questions to which answers will have to be found when we have got past the stage of the experimental introduction of self-directed learning systems and in the light of those experiences.

4. Conclusions: structural consequences

There are two overall educational situations that will arise in the future:

4.1. The first situation will be that in which autonomous learners will find themselves (whether this autonomy has been achieved 'naturally' or 'systematically'). For such the learning structure will from the outset need to be a self-directed one, organized therefore by reference to their specific learning needs. It may be imagined that in a structure of this sort there will be a large and assorted body of informants of all kinds, both human and technical and that there will be a technological infrastructure capable of temporarily making up for deficiencies in individual technological means, etc.

4.2. However, the most prevalent situation will be that of learners who are not yet autonomous but are involved in the process of acquiring the ability to assume responsibility for their learning.

In this situation the learning structure will be made up of a maximum (as regards quantity and variety) of both human and technical supports.

4.3. In both these situations, however, it will be essential for the learning structure regularly to supply the learners with all the information that will be of benefit to them in their learning, whether they be autonomous or not:

[8] Janne, H, *op cit*, p 18.

— information on language needs in the world outside (in society) such as may be needed by a learner when making decisions as to his objectives;

— information on the processes of acquiring second languages such as will help the learner to arrive at a better definition of his methods and techniques and his learning procedure;

— information on verbal communication, the psychological and social dimensions of which need to be considered by a learner when defining objectives and evaluation processes;

— information on available documentation which the learner will use for defining contents.

It will thus be necessary to set up systems that are both very diversified, in order to take into account the broad range of knowledge, and very dynamic in order to keep pace with the development of this knowledge and of the world outside. It is in this direction also that consideration and research will need to move in the years ahead if we wish to develop autonomous learning.

At present, a number of more or less comprehensive experiments concerning the autonomy of learning have already been launched. We shall describe some of these experiments in the next chapter in order, if possible, to single out some hypothetical models that could form the basis for future learning systems.

IV. EXPERIMENTS

Our purpose in this chapter is not to describe all the experiments now in progress which have the express aim of introducing learning on an autonomous basis: apart from the fact that in some of them 'autonomy' means no more than 'absence of a teacher', our object is merely to describe some examples of what is being done so as to illustrate in a practical fashion how the introduction of self-directed learning may be expected to take place.

1. The Stirling experiment (Great Britain)

As part of a summer course intended for foreign teachers of English (at secondary and higher levels) the British Council arranged a self-directed type 'finishing' language structure at the University of Stirling in August 1978.

Within this structure the students were supplied with:
— support provided by the teachers;
— a quantity of learning materials (courses and other authentic matter).

1.1.   The support provided by the teachers was intended to help the learners to define their objectives, choose suitable learning materials and evaluate what they acquired.

It was made available in the shape of a five-part questionnaire[1] handed to each learner:

(a) Time availability: the questions helped the learner to determine as exactly as possible the amount of time he would necessarily have to spend on study and so work out the weekly time allowance to be devoted to language learning.

(b) Methods of assessment: the questions helped the learner to decide what means would be available to him for assessing his progress.

(c) Work priorities: the questions helped the learner determine his learning needs by considering five different areas ("speaking English", "understanding and using spoken English", "developing vocabulary", "reading" and "writing"), how far competence in each of these areas was "necessary/desirable/not necessary" in his own case, what was his level in each area ("must improve/would like to improve/OK") and the order of priority as regards area and the amount of time he was prepared to give to study of each area;

(d) A list of information setting out for each of the areas mentioned in the previous paragraph the materials available to the learner with suggestions on means of assessing what he has correspondingly acquired.

(e) A bibliography.

The aim of the questionnaire was thus to assist the learner to consider how to define his learning needs, choose his materials and assess his progress.

---

[1] *cf* Appendix I.

1.2.   The materials for use in learning were made available to the students in the shape of a library of sound recordings, the physical organization of which was attended to by a teacher.

1.3.   With respect to the self-directed nature of learning in this structure we find that:

(a) the learner continues to be in charge of all decisions relating to the definition of objectives and contents, monitoring of learning procedure and assessment;

(b) but the framework within which those decisions are made is limited by the teachers:

— analysis of learning needs is carried out strictly in the terms set out in the questionnaire (five areas subdivided into a small number of aspects); the questionnaire does in fact include a section for "Other areas" which theoretically allows the learner to specify other needs but in practice he can use this section only provided he knows how to analyse his needs (and the sections described in the questionnaire will not teach him how to do that);

— the materials from which he can make his choice are strictly defined and correspond to the range of those which the teaching establishment can offer him; he is never given any opportunity, nor is it even suggested to him, of discovering material for himself and thus his own personal types of activity;

(c) but, in the same way, the learning methods and techniques prescribed for him are those of the materials suggested to him.

This is therefore an interesting but incomplete experiment in self-directed learning.

2.   The Bournemouth Eurocentre experiment (Great Britain)

2.1.   This experiment relates to continuous self-assessment of oral communicative skills with support and aims at the future introduction of a self-assessment process as part of a system of instruction centred on the learner.

The structure employed includes courses in which the teacher and the teaching play their 'traditional' roles but also proposes to the learners the beginnings of learning on an autonomous basis centred on assessment.

2.2.   This learning of self-assessment is done by means of a number of activities[2] enabling the learner to achieve performances in which he makes use of the knowledge he has been able to acquire in the part of the curriculum which he is assessing.

Assessment of those performances is then done by the learner with help from the teacher and other learners with the twofold purpose:
— of discovering and learning to use assessment criteria;
— of realizing what progress has been made and deciding on future learning activities.

[2] cf Appendix II.

28

2.3.   The content of this experiment calls for a few comments:

(a) Learning self-assessment is regarded by those in charge of the experiment not as an end in itself but as one stage in the development of the learner's autonomy: the ultimate aim of the institution ('the light at the end of the tunnel' as they say) is to introduce a system in which the learner will assume responsibility for his learning as he learns how to learn.

(b) Assessment is chosen as a first stage for two main reasons:

— it represents a crucial level of learning and consequently of acceptance of responsibility for learning;

— it is closely bound up with the objectives which, in the context of the Bournemouth Eurocentre, are to a large extent identical for all the learners (ability to live in a country and not professional or vocational requirements). This quasi-identical nature of learning objectives thus facilitates group learning of self-assessment.

(c) There are some dangers involved in the techniques used for learning self-assessment:

— the learners are constantly led to compare their own assessments with those made by the other learners and the teacher and in the absence of certain precautions this may strengthen or even give rise to the idea that there is one correct assessment and one only and that subjective assessment is not acceptable unless it comes close to a presumed 'objective' assessment; and this is an idea incompatible with the concept of self-assessment;

— the assessment tools offered to the learner are of a 'school' type and can be used only in a 'school' situation; they do not fit the learner sufficiently to carry out self-assessment in a real situation and thus to check that his learning objectives actually correspond to his communicative objectives.

The interesting part of this experiment is that it shows how it is possible to introduce self-direction of learning into a 'traditional' system of teaching in a limited but real way.

3.   The Study Circles experiment in Sweden

The study circles system is one of comprehensive learning designed to encourage education for the masses.

"Through them the state finances the free organization by citizens and their organizations (associations, trade unions, political parties, churches) of any educational activity which brings together a sufficient number of people to justify the existence of a study group. A vast free educational service is thus made operational; the only restriction imposed by the state is administrative (number of people per group, educational content, duration, quality of the teaching and leadership)"[3]

---

[3] Scheffknecht, JJ, in Schualtz, B(1977) *Permant education.* Work of Consolidation of the Evaluation of Pilot Experiments in the Permanent Education Field, CCC/EP (77) 3, p 102.

3.1.   This is a *self-directed* system of learning; it includes neither courses nor traditional teachers, each circle organizing its own learning with the help of an *animateur* whose role is not to teach but to "organize the group, see that it has the necessary material means, promote discussion and cooperative work".[4]

3.2.   Acceptance of responsibility must be carried out by the group (the participants and the *animateur*): thus it is for the group to define its objectives, contents, methods and techniques, the learning procedure (number and length of sessions) and make an assessment of what has been learned. This pre-supposes either that the learners are autonomous and therefore capable of accepting this responsibility or else that the *animateur* is going to help them achieve this autonomy.

3.3.   In practice it is found that self-directed learning is not, so to speak, guaranteed and the group very quickly organizes itself on the lines of a traditional school system with the *animateur* acting as teacher and a course built up in the form of a learning support: the learner's part is confined to choosing a textbook in accordance with criteria that vary from one study circle to another but which are generally not very satisfactory in that neither learning objectives, nor contents, nor methods and techniques have been properly decided upon in advance.

This situation is a direct result of the fact that:
(a) the learners are not autonomous when they start a study circle;
(b) owing to lack of training the *animateurs* are not capable of providing the support they should for members of the circle who are not autonomous.[5]

4.   Experiments at the Centre de Recherches et d'Applications Pédagogiques en Langues (Nancy, France)

4.1.   *The system of learning on an autonomous basis*

Since 1974 CRAPEL at the University of Nancy II has been using a self-directed learning structure with support designed to take learners who cannot or do not wish to follow a set course.[6] Its two-fold aim is to provide training in self-directed learning and training in a language (English) and it covers:
— *animateurs* whose duties are to provide the support needed in order to become autonomous;

[4] Chaix, P and C O'Neil (1978) *Etude critique des modalités d'apprentissage autonome (autodidaxie et semi-autonomie) dans le domaine de l'acquisition des langues vivants secondes—Rapport de synthèse* UNESCO ED/78/WS/58, May 1978, Chapter VIII, edited by M Candelier (NB Autonomy in this document means 'absence of teacher').

[5] It is to be hoped that with the present tendency to turn the *animateur* into a 'professional' the direction taken as far as the role of *animateur* is concerned will not result in language study circles becoming purely and simply language courses.

[6] A detailed description of this structure and the way it works will be found in Henner-Stanchina, C (1976) *Autonomy: a viable strategy for adult language learners* Degree thesis, University of Nancy II.

— learning materials made available to the learners;
— a collection of sound and video recordings;
— native speakers.

4.1.1.   Acceptance of responsibility for the learning is individual and total: each learner defines his own objectives, contents, methods and techniques and the manner in which his learning is done and assesses his own attainments. In this he is helped by an *animateur* with whom he can make an appointment as often as he wants; the content of their interviews has reference to the learning process and is never a 'course' either in methods or language: his meeting with the *animateur* gives the learner an opportunity to think about his learning (to define needs and initial aims, then to consider the methods and techniques he is using now and those he intends to employ in the future, and his self-assessment) in order to develop the abilities he needs in order to be able to take over responsibility for his learning.

4.1.2.   The materials made available to the learner include 'courses' produced by CRAPEL or obtainable on the market, teaching 'modules' constructed for learning on an autonomous basis and authentic materials of all kinds. They form the complete range of working materials from which the learner chooses his own contents at the start of his studies if he has none of his own to suggest.

Later on he will add his own contributions to this range whenever possible.

Selection of learning contents is generally made 'by trial and error'.

4.1.3.   The native speakers[7] play their part by supplying information at the learner's request but also by conversing with him to help him learn communicative skills (oral expression) and by acting as 'developers' for self-assessment.[8]

4.1.4.   This is therefore a comprehensive self-directed system of learning intended for learners who are not yet autonomous.

4.2. Group self-tuition

In 1977–1978 CRAPEL introduced a group self-tuition structure for the public attending the University of Nancy for senior citizens and others with available free time.[9]

This is a special use of the principle of self-directed learning for an audience for which the group system is indispensable.

The structure covers:
— *animateurs* whose role is to assist groups of learners to assume responsibility for their studies;
— learning materials;
— a collection of sound and video recordings;
— native speakers.

[7] English or American people who are not teachers.

[8] *cf* Henner-Stanchina, C, and Holec, H, *op cit.*

[9] A detailed description of this experiment will be found in Sicre, M (1978) *Une expérience d'auto-enseignement de groupe en anglais (Public du IIIème âge)* Degree thesis, University of Nancy II.

4.2.1.   Responsibility for organizing the learning is in the hands of the group (ten to fifteen people). After a general introduction to methods at the start of the year in the shape of five consecutive full half-day sessions devoted to a consideration of this subject, each group (composed of the learners themselves) defines its objectives and the learning procedure (the weekly timetables decided upon at the beginning of the year may be altered, within the limits imposed by availability of the premises). The first sessions are given over to looking at the available materials; later on each group decides upon the contents needed by it for each session.

4.2.2.   The *animateurs* take no part in the groups unless called upon. The meetings are devoted to considering the type of learning suitable to help the learners in their search for methods and techniques and means of self-assessment.

4.2.3.   The groups appeal to native speakers when they wish to do so and decide for themselves what subjects shall be dealt with on such occasions.[10]

4.2.4.   This is therefore a comprehensive self-directed system of learning intended for learners who are not autonomous but including group and not individual acceptance of responsibility.

5.   Conclusions — Future developments

The few experiments we have just briefly described provide some very useful information on developments in learning on an autonomous basis and the possibilities for introducing suitable systems. In particular they show that for the time being it is by no means essential to replace existing teaching systems *en bloc* by new ones but that, on the contrary, the educational dynamism as represented by autonomy renders it possible to use the existing systems, modified as necessary, as a preparation for self-directed learning. Obviously such preparation is necessary (as proved by the relative failure of 'study circles' in this field):

> ". . . the promoters of self-management in education must be realistic and proceed carefully. Introducing self-management demands preparation: the idea might seem paradoxical except that it implies transforming an awareness into a reality by experience, before any institutional implementation".[11]

The manner of carrying out such preparation will need to be investigated through experimental research similar to that we have described.

For the time being experience shows that there are two broad developments that can be visualized:

(a) a movement in the direction of introducing comprehensive self-managed systems of learning parallel with the existing systems of teaching:

— this development would enable immediate consideration to be given to learners learners who do not fit into a system of teaching without at the same time obliging all the rest to adopt a similar course;

— it would also provide opportunities for empirical, *gradual* search for solutions to the problems involved in autonomy as regards both learners and teachers;

---

[10] The only instruction given to native speakers is not to 'teach'. Here again they are English speakers who are not teachers.

[11] Janne, H, *op cit*, p 31.

— in the case of group self-direction these learning systems would be sufficiently similar on the institutional side to existing systems of teaching as not to involve too great a change and lead to 'blockages' at all levels of the institution;

(b) a movement in the direction of introducing evolutionary mixed systems based on existing systems of teaching, the gradual introduction into those systems of teaching of self-directed learning as carried out (in Bournemouth, for example) by means of graduated training towards autonomy for the learners with learning support provided by the teachers without any radical alteration in the institutional structure; such a movement would enable the concept of learner-centredness to be taken beyond what are insuperable barriers for the individualization of teaching and to deal in an increasingly satisfactory way with the manifold differences between adult audiences.

V. GENERAL CONCLUSIONS

In this study we have touched on the analysis of the concepts of autonomy on the part of the learner and self-directed learning from the standpoint of the learner, the teacher and the teaching establishment in an attempt to describe the many practical implications of the application of these concepts to language learning by adults. Although incomplete, the picture thus obtained shows, when translated into practical educational terms, the specific features of action 'on an autonomous basis', the essential characteristic of which is that it is an act of learning, and not of teaching, done by the learner and not the teacher. This reversal of the educational situation poles involves redefining all the functional components of that situation.

Two conclusions of a general nature will enable us to bring this study to a close.

1. The first is concerned with the implications of the process on the individual and on society. Self-directed language learning is essentially similar to self-directed education generally and the latter in turn is part of self-directed overall social behaviour. From one point of view therefore, autonomy in an individual in one of these spheres cannot be dissociated from his autonomy in other areas, and the problem that arises is one both of accountability on the part of the individual as between acceptance of responsibility in language learning and in the rest of his affairs, and the problem, so far as society is concerned, of accountability as between educational responsibility and responsibility as regards occupation, politics, and so on. Can an individual 'live' in a state of partial autonomy such as would relate solely to his learning of languages in a general environment of dependence and passivity? May we not think that "the various organizational elements by which our life-setting is structured . . . have a more decisive effect upon our possibilities for development than does either training or education?"[1] Thus we are faced with the whole problem of the 'success' of autonomy.

2. The second consideration, allied to the first but of a more practical nature, is concerned with the institutional attitude to be adopted towards autonomization. In this context a distinction has to be made between 'autonomy' and 'self-direction' in learning. Although autonomy, ie the ability to assume responsibility for one's learning, must definitely be one of the objectives of every adult training establishment — and this despite all the difficulties which its introduction involves — self-direction in learning must remain a possibility offered to and not forced upon the learners, "a tendency to be encouraged"[2] and, let us add, *prepared*. For the time being therefore there is no question of wishing to force the learner to assume responsibility for his learning at all costs, and there probably never will be; what must be developed is the learner's ability to assume this responsibility. It is in this direction, we believe, that it is essential to develop language teaching/learning systems for adults.

[1] Schwartz, B (1977) CCC/EP (77) 8 revised, p 12.
[2] Trim, J L M, *op cit*, p 8.

APPENDIX I
SELF-DIRECTED LEARNING
IN ENGLISH AS A
FOREIGN LANGUAGE—
AIMS AND OBJECTIVES
QUESTIONNAIRE
UNIVERSITY OF STIRLING, GREAT BRITAIN

W D Cousin   R Dauer   L Dickinson   C J Moore

In attempting to map out a course of any sort of self-improvement nothing is so frustrating as setting oneself unrealistic aims. You may set out with a great deal of enthusiasm but find (a) that the task is more difficult than you thought (b) you never seem to have enough time.

The first may stem from difficulties in assessment — firstly, making an accurate assessment of where you actually stand, and secondly, devising a method of assessment which will be sensitive enough to register your progress. Your progress may, after all, be quite limited!

The second cause of frustration, the lack of time, stems from a very natural tendency to suppose life is going to be suddenly very different, now you have decided to learn. This is a dangerous assumption and careful analysis of the extent of your unchanging commitments (to sleep, for instance!) may give you a very different idea of what is feasible.

In the most usual situation for learning anything, you have a teacher whose profession it is to be aware of these sources of frustration and guide you and encourage you in your difficulties. But where you are to be your own teacher it is very important to make up your programme having thought carefully about what, in the end, you are likely to achieve.

It is the purpose of this questionnaire to help you with that preliminary thinking.

1.   Time availability

It is always difficult to think objectively about how you spend your time. It is even more difficult to think of descriptions of human activities which are applicable to the many different situations in which people live and work. The following list of categories is a compromise which will, hopefully, meet most people's requirements without being too embarrassingly personal.

You may be using this questionnaire within a tightly structured programme so that your responses to some questions may not be 'normal' for you in your home background. For this reason, a column has been left blank for you to fill in the picture for your home programme in case you want to plan your work later.

Clearly not all days are the same and it is sometimes difficult to make averages. It is probably simplest to think of what happens on a typical day.

How much time do you spend each day on average on the following (be honest!)

Time

Activity	1st Assessment	2nd Assessment	Home
(a)			
i. Sleeping			
ii. Getting up			
(b) Eating			
i. Preparing for and eating three main meals			
ii. Short breaks (snacks, coffee, etc)			
(c) Work			
i. Your main routine commitment in office or classroom — the 9–5, or whatever, day			
ii. Travel to and from work			
iii. Preparation for work (at home)			

You will probably find on your first assessment that you either (a) have long hours in the day when you appear to do absolutely nothing or (b) there are not enough hours in the day for all you do!

If (a) is your problem try taking a typical day and thinking through *everything* you do. Have you perhaps not allowed enough time for *preparing* for eating meals?

(At one end of the scale it is a matter of peeling the potatoes, while at the other end, Victorian Britishers used actually to 'dress for dinner', an hour, an hour and a half?) Use the column marked 2nd Assessment.

If (b) is your problem this probably reflects the inclusion of activities which you would normally only undertake say once or twice a week. Try taking a typical day and fill out the column under 2nd Assessment to get the balance of time right. But bear in mind the different activities that *might* fill up your time.

Now you are probably in a position to think which of these activities you can do without. And don't forget that you *are* going to have to give something up. And don't choose sleep. That is only a *very* short solution, or you will soon have to be short-term/ timetabling fifteen minutes here and there in the afternoon for the times you doze off!

You can organize your work on a daily or a weekly basis. Of course everyone is different, but it is probably not worth scheduling less than half an hour at any one time. And it is probably unrealistic to schedule more than two hours at any one time. Few of us get even that long undisturbed.

Now work out your *weekly* time allowance and multiply it by the length of time your course will run in weeks.

☐	hours

☐	weeks

Total:	☐	hours

That is the total number of hours you have for study. Does it surprise you?

2. Methods of Assessment

The first question to be asked under this heading is clearly:

(a) i. Are you working for an examination? ☐

Your calculation of the time you have to study in may make you think carefully about whether preparation for a public examination is really feasible in the time available.

However, if you *are* working for an examination you can further ask:

ii. Are previous papers available? ☐

iii. Do the papers equate with my objectives? ☐

iv. If not *how* can I equate them?
     (What *courses* could I follow?)

However, whether or not you are working for a public examination you may want to consider some ways in which you can measure your progress towards your aim. Here there are basically two considerations:

i. the availability of test material.
ii. the availability of people to *assess* your efforts.

Under (i) you might like to consider:

(b) i. Are the materials programmed? ☐

ii. Do the learning materials themselves contain any tests? ☐

iii. Can you set aside some tests to measure progress at a later date? ☐

iv. Can you devise a description of the criterion (critical behaviour) at which you are aiming (what *exactly* it is you want to be able to do)? ☐

v. Can you devise tests like the ones in your course of the same criterion? ☐

vi. Are there any published tests relevant to your materials? ☐

vii. Are there any informal test situations that will measure the criterion (eg does a native speaker react to you more or less like another native speaker, do you understand the same thing as a native speaker from a leader in *The Times*/a BBC news broadcast)?

viii. Can you make use of a 'cloze' test? (In a cloze test you delete words — eg every seventh — and then try to replace them. It can be done with any material, for example with newspaper. All you have to do is to cut out or paste over the words and then photocopy.)

Under (ii) the availability of people to assess your efforts, you might like to consider:

(c)   i. Can I make use of the judgement of a native speaker?
(A) An expert
(B) A peer (student like myself)?
    ii. Can I make use of the judgement of a non-native speaker?
(A) An expert
(B) A peer like myself?
    iii. Can I devise a way of getting someone to judge my level of achievement?

(This is like the problem of criterion above— what *exactly* is the other person supposed to notice/*not* to notice eg will he/she accept your right to 'buy a round' in a pub as a member of the (perhaps native-speaking) group? Does the shopkeeper *assume* that you know the conventions that govern what you can buy where in Britain or does he obviously feel the need to explain (ie as to a *foreigner*)!)

    iv. Can you devise situations where you can test this out (eg can you get a group/ your informant to accept a recording you have made as from a native speaker? Can native speakers detect your country of origin, and so on).

3.   Work priorities (access to materials on pages indicated)

For each of the following areas consider the following questions:

(a) How necessary is this area for my work? (Necessary/desirable/not necessary)

(b) What is my level (Must improve/Would like to improve/OK)

(c) What order or priority would I give it? (Place any number of areas that interest you in order.)

(d) How much time can I give this? (Remember the results of the previous analysis!)

When you have decided on your priorities go to the page indicated which will guide you to materials. (The abbreviations are explained in the bibliography at the back).

When you have found materials give some thought to how you might assess your progress. In some areas suggestions are made, but you may be able to devise methods of your own (see 2 above).

In some areas you may even wish to consider whether assessment is appropriate. Or even possible?

Area	Access	Necessary	Desirable	Not necessary	Must improve	Like to improve	OK	Priority	Time available
1. Speaking English									
1.1. Correct model (particular sounds)	p 40								
1.2. Fluency	p 40								
1.3. Nuance (intonation)	p 40								
2. Understanding and using spoken English									
2.1. Formal style	p 40								
2.2. Conversational style	p 40								
2.3. Accent and dialect	p 41								
2.4. Focussing on meaning (accuracy)	p 41								
3. Developing vocabulary									
3.1. Appropriacy (style)	p 41								
3.2. Passive made active vocabulary	p 41								
3.3. Acquire now (eg register)	p 41								
3.4. Group language development	p 41								
4. Reading									
4.1. Speed	p 41								
4.2. Strategies (see also 3 above)	p 41								
5. Writing English									
5.1. Quality	p 42								
5.2 Accuracy	p 42								
5.3. Construction	p 42								
5.4. Purpose	p 42								
5.5. Economy	p 43								
6. Other									

Area heading	Access to materials	Assessment
1. Speaking English		
1.1. Correct model		
1.1.1. Vowels Do you make the difference between 'seat' and 'sit', 'hat' and 'hot', 'hurt' and 'hut' (Try them on your friends!)	Look under appropriate headings (or index) in: Trim *English pronunciation illustrated* Gimson *A practical course* Hill *Drills and tests* Mortimer *Sounds right* O'Connor *Better English pronunciation*	Try them on your friends. Better, make up critical sentences and try them on native speakers (but think what *else* the native speaker might be listening to/hearing) Best, pass for a native in a pub or other situation.
1.1.2. Consonants Do you make the difference between 'rich' and 'ridge', 'taught' and 'thought', 'rebel' and 'revel', 'seats' and 'seeds' (Try them on your friends!)		
1.2. Fluency	Mortimer *Link up* Allen *Living English speech* MacArthur *Natural speech*	As above or try tape recording and attempting to get native speaker to accept it as from another native speaker.
1.2.1. Linking		
1.2.2. Contraction and weak forms	Mortimer *Contractions* Mortimer *Weak forms* Gimson Allen	
1.2.3. Stress placement	Allen, McArthur, Gimson	
1.2.4. Rhythm	Mortimer *Stress Time* Allen	
1.2.5. Vowel and syllable length	Allen O'Connor	
1.3 Nuance (intonation)		
1.3.1. Choice of tonic (tonicity)	Halliday *A course in spoken English intonation*	Try changing the tones when speaking to a native speaker and see if you can confuse him! (Choose your moment!)
1.3.2. Choice of tone contour (tone)	Allen McArthur Cook *Active intonation* Gimson	
1.3.3. Discourse	Brazil *Discourse intonation*	
2. Understanding and using spoken English		
2.1 Formal style (lectures, written text spoken)	SRA *Listening materials* Lectures Authentic lectures (see also under Vocabulary)	Note-taking. Reconstitute from notes.
2.2 Conversational style	Coles and Lord	Authentic conversations with native speakers.
2.2.1. Idiom	*Colloquial English* (see also Vocabulary) Alexander *Question and Answer* O'Keefe *People overhead, Points overhead* Ockenden *Situational dialogues*	
2.2.2. Indirect constructions (for politeness etc)	Mortimer *Phrasal verbs*	Collect — try out as appropriate.

Area heading	Access to materials	Assessment
2.3. Accent and dialect	Dickinson and Mackin *Varieties of spoken English* Dickinson and Mackin A few recordings of dialect Authentic Scottish Dickinson *News from Newcastle* Mawson and Wareham *Larn yersel Geordie* Tom McArthur *Introducing Scots* 3 North-American Dialect Speakers	
2.4. Focussing on meaning (accuracy) Accuracy	Dickinson and Mackin Note-taking materials Barrett *Success with English* O'Neill *Kernel lessons* Intermediate and *Kernel lessons plus* Jerrom and Szkitnik *Conversation exercises in everyday English*	
3. Developing vocabulary (decide which material you want to work with: Professional Media Novels and stories Non-fiction, non-professional)	Library Newspapers Library SRA	Depends on area chosen below.
3.1. Appropriacy	Look at differences in style eg in listening materials above	Try out preferably with native speakers.
3.2. Passive made active vocabulary	Discuss reading material eg SRA with colleagues	
3.3. Acquire now (eg register)	Look for appropriate register in eg newspapers, library Use authentic texts to make cloze tests	Keep some cloze tests. Do again after a few days.
3.4. Group language development	Various simulation schemes eg *Nine graded situations*	
4. Reading		
4.1. Speed	SRA Rate Builders de Leeuw *Read better, Read faster* (see above under vocabulary)	Built-in. Built-in.
4.2. Strategies	Fischer *Reading to discover organization* Yorkey *Study skills*	

Area heading	Access to materials	Assessment

5. Writing English

5.1. Quality: this means appreciating how to use the correct language for the correct situation. You may have your own aims here, and should make them known to the tutor. If you want a starting point, it is suggested that you undertake a close comparison between formal and informal letter-writing styles in English.

Formal letter style: 'open' letters on notice boards, etc and letters to newspapers (*The Times, Daily Telegraph*), letters you may have received in English in connection with this course.

Informal style: Jupp and Milne pp 36 and 71, letters from English friends, library: collections of private letters or examples in biographies etc.

Having listed what you consider to be the main points of stylistic difference, apply your criteria more broadly, initially to further written material, and finally to your own attempts at composition.

5.2. Accuracy: this means grammatical competence in general, and for most people this can be reduced to eliminating errors in points of grammar.

For checking points of grammar and general reference:
Quirk *et al.*
Thompson and Martinet
Leech and Svartvik

For finding out the main differences between written and spoken English, and for practising indirect address: Arapoff, Section 1, pp 1–73.

For general practice in structures, especially in the context of composition: Jupp and Milne

Access to a native speaker is the surest way of identifying errors in grammatical usage. Try to get a native speaker to mark errors in your work without correcting them. Find out *what* is wrong yourself.

5.3. Construction: this means manipulating the functions and relations between propositions — the building bricks with which composition is achieved.

For improving knowledge of language about language, and its functions:
Lawrence, pp 13–39
Coulthard, all.
Halliday and Hasan, all.
Fries, all.
The last three texts are for those who are ready for a slightly more complex level of linguistic discussion.

For practising functional relations in writing:
Arapoff, pp 75–188

For putting information into words:
Lawrence, Level 1;
Level 2;
Level 3;

For practice in paragraph writing through functions:
Imhoof and Hudson.

Most of these materials are designed for self-study and provide their own assessment.

Once you are familiar with some of the ideas, try to read more analytically in your daily exposure to other books, newspapers, etc.

5.4. Purpose: this means organizing one's composition so as to achieve an intended effect. The formal report may be taken as a good example to work with. Make other suggestions.

For planning and laying out a report effectively:
Heaton.

Start to prepare a report on the course itself for your return home. Work with others and test your ideas against one another.

Area heading	*Access to materials*	*Assessment*
5.5. *Economy:* this means finding out how to use language in the briefest possible way is a means of communicating or recording information.	For practice in summarizing: Arapoff, Section III Yorkey, Chapter 4. For advice on how to take notes: Heaton. Yorkey, Chapter 6.	Start to take notes during supervised sessions. Look at your notes later and attempt to write them out again more fully. Read magazine articles and then write summaries from memory or from notes. Check your summary against the original.

Bibliography

Alexander, L G (1968) *Question and answer* Longman.

Alexander, L G (1967) *Practice and progress* Longman.

Allen, W Stannard (1954, 1977) *Living English Speech* Longman.

Arapoff, Nancy (1970) *Writing through understanding* Holt, Rinehart & Winston.

BBC (1971) *English with a dialect* BBC Publications.

Brazil, David (1975, 1978) Discourse intonation *English Language Research* Birmingham University.

Broughton, G (1969) *Success with English* Books 1, 2, 3. Penguin.

Coles, M C, and B Lord (1970) *Colloquial English* Oxford University Press.

Cook, V J (1968) *Active intonation* Longman.

Coulthard, M (1977) *An introduction to discourse analysis* Longman.

de Leeuw, M and E (1965) *Read better, read faster* Penguin.

Dickinson, L (1974) *News from Newcastle* Mary Glasgow.

Dickinson, L, and R Mackin (1969) *Varieties of spoken English* Oxford University Press.

Dobson, S (nd) *Larn yersel Geordie* Mawson and Wareham, Newcastle (Record no. MWN 1001S, F Graham, 1970).

Fisher, J A (1969) *Reading to discover organization* (Basic Skills System) McGraw Hill.

Fries, C C (1957) *The structure of English* Longman.

Gimson, A C (1975) *A practical course of English pronunciation* Edward Arnold.

Halliday, M A K (1970) *A course in spoken English intonation* Oxford University Press.

Halliday, M A K, and R Hasan (1976) *Cohesion in English* Longman.

Heaton, J B (1978) *Studying in English* Longman.

Hill, L A (1967) *Drills and tests with English sounds* Longman.

Imhoof, M, and H Hudson (1975) *From paragraph to essay* Longman.

Jupp, T C, and J Milne (1969) *Guided course in English composition* Heinemann.

Lawrence, M (1972) *Writing as a thinking process* University of Michigan Press.

Leech, G, and J Svartvik (1975) *A communicative grammar of English* Longman.

Lewis, J Windsor (1977) *People speaking* Oxford University Press.

MacArthur, T (1975) *Natural speech* Scotsway (Longniddry) & Un. of Edinburgh Department of Extra-Mural Studies.

MacArthur, T (1977) *Introducing Scots* Scotsway (Longniddry) & Un. of Edinburgh Department of Extra-Mural Studies.

MacArthur, T, and M Heliel (1974) *Learning rhythm and stress* Collins.

Mackenzie, M D M (1967) *Modern English pronunciation practice* Longman.

Mortimer, Colin (1972) *Phrasal verbs in conversation* Longman.

Mortimer, Colin (1975) *Sounds right* Longman.

Mortimer, Colin (1) *Stress time* (1976), (2) *Weak forms* (1977), (3) *Contractions* (1977), (4) *Link up* (1977) (Cambridge English Language Learning Series) Cambridge University Press.

Nine graded situations (1975) Inner London Education Authority Media Resources Centre.

Ockenden, H (1972) *Situational dialogues* Longman.

O'Connor, J D (1967) *Better English pronunciation* Cambridge University Press.

O'Keefe (1975) (1) *People overheard* (2) *Points overheard* Macmillan.

O'Neill, R, *et al* (1971) *Kernel lessons intermediate* Longman.

O'Neill, R, *et al* (1973/4) *Kernel lessons plus* Longman.

Quirk, R, *et al* (1975) *A grammar of contemporary English* Longman.

Science Research Associates (SRA) (1) *Reading lab. IIIb* (1963), (2) *Reading lab. 4a* (1959), (3) *Reading for understanding: senior* (1980) (4) *Research lab* (1974) Science Research Associates, Chicago, Henley-on-Thames, Paris.

Thomson, A J, and A Martinet (1962) *A practical English grammar* Oxford University Press.

Three North American dialect speakers (nd) National Council of Teachers of English, Urbana, Illinois.

Trim, J L M (1975) *English pronunciation illustrated* Cambridge University Press.

Yorkey, Richard C (1970) *Study skills for students of English as a foreign language* McGraw Hill.

APPENDIX II
MODELS FOR THE SELF-ASSESSMENT OF ORAL COMMUNICATIVE SKILLS AND THEIR FUNCTIONS

by

D. Ferris

Eurocentre, Bournemouth, United Kingdom

General remarks

The reliability of the students' assessments in any given model will depend upon whether previous training has put them in a position to succeed in the task set and then make a fairly reliable assessment. This is turn depends upon creating a supportive atmosphere in the group, where they can look upon each other and their teachers as helpers rather than judges. It follows that the models used should be ordered so that they move progressively from highly structured situations, where confidence can be built, to freer situations which approximate more closely to real life.

The models and their uses

(a) Laboratory follow-up to oral practice lessons

Aim

To enable the student to assess the progress he has made in a simple transaction in relation to a few focal points that he has practised with his teacher. The activity gives him models in the areas of fluency, intonation and pronunciation which help him to internalize criteria for assessing his performance.

Activity

After students have been taught about three units from our oral practice material, they act out a simple transaction in pairs and record it.

Example: You see a new student in class:
(A) Introduce yourself.
(B) Answer.

They then take off their earphones and the teacher focuses on just a few points relating to fluency (catenation and sentence stress), intonation and pronunciation and practises them with the class live. If the class cannot remember the words, then progressive fading using an overhead projector can be used. After this practice the students are given a sheet with the focal points indicated on it. They re-record the interaction. After this they compare their first version with the second and try to be specific about the

45

progress they have made in relation to the focal points. They make notes under two categories:

1. What you said.
2. How you said it.

They can record again if they are still dissatisfied with their second performance. The advantage of comparing their first version to their second after their practice is that the student becomes aware of progress and is encouraged. This is not usually the case if he always compares himself with a native speaker as in most laboratory drills because the performance gap is often dishearteningly large for a beginner.

Conclusion

The students' assessment in pairs is quite reliable because they can look at certain discrete points one at a time having just practised them with the teacher. They felt a sense of achievement with this activity because progress was easy to see even for the weak student who may do no more than get the words more or less right in the second version but may have been inarticulate in the first version. They did become aware of some of the criteria involved in assessing their own performances.

(b) Oral homework

Aim

To consolidate what has been learnt in class, help the students to form clearer concepts of the criteria for assessment and their progress through the course by comparing various transactions recorded at different stages.

Activity

Students work on recording a version of a few simple transactions that seem satisfactory to them for as long as they decide to.

Example: You are in a new town:
(A) Ask where a place is.
(B) Say where the place is.
(A) Thank the first person.
(B) Answer the thanks.

The teacher tries to supply as much guidance as is needed by the students, which initially is quite considerable, because the students do not know how to go about the task and lack confidence. The weaker students do simple written work with faded dialogues for the first few weeks till they have established a basis for oral production. The students like to write out their dialogues first, and then practice reading them until they feel ready to record. They listen to their recording and ask themselves the two questions:

1. Did I use the right words?
2. How did I say it?

If they can identify any points for improvement they can record again and again until they are satisfied or their patience gives out. The teacher can go through their tape with them after they have finished and after telling them what they have done well, show them one or two points that they could further improve. Each pair keeps his own cassette and when they record other transactions again in about three weeks' time can listen to their previous performance and assess general progress in general areas like fluency and pronunciation.

Conclusion

The reliability of the students' judgement tends to improve and become more refined with time. In answering the question "was the oral homework useful for you? Why?" all answered "yes". Some of the reasons given were:

1. We could learn more as we worked on it, and thought of more things.
2. We had to concentrate more than in just written work and this helped us to remember better.
3. It helped us to do self-study, to do more for ourselves and to think for ourselves.
4. It was important to practice with another person.
5. We could use the things we learnt outside the school.

The standards of performance achieved by the students were well above the level achieved when they did paired work in class when they first did a unit. They also expressed more of their personality as they could work together in private.

(c) Group evaluation of oral homework

Aim

To train the whole group to evaluate together and establish standards for the class. To motivate them by comparing previous levels of performance with the present level and identifying the progress made. To get members of the group to help their fellow students and advise them where they can further improve their performance.

Activity

Tapes of oral homework are played to the class. Each student has to make his own assessment in two areas (1) words used (2) how it was said. He indicates his assessment by holding up one of four cards 1 = very good; 2 = good; 3 = acceptable; 4 = needs more work. After the cards are shown to the teacher there is a discussion as to why assessments were arrived at and advice is given in a helpful way to the student who was assessed.

Conclusion

This activity should not be tried unless the group know each other well and are prepared to be supportive to each other. We tried it after about eight weeks with a particularly friendly group and it went very well. About 80% of the class came up with assessments that corresponded to that of the teacher which meant that the previous training had helped. The class were particularly sensitive to the social aspects of the transaction and reacted if an inappropriate expression or intonation pattern was used. They indicated this awareness by awarding half bonus marks if they felt someone's intonation was particularly appropriate.

(d) Half-term and end-of-term oral test

Aims

For the class to assess themselves in the functions covered to date and identify where remedial work is to be done. Those who had attained mastery in certain areas would help their colleagues in those areas.

Activity

Between six to eight cue cards are given to each student in advance so that he can prepare all of them for the test. A model tape using native speakers is provided for each transaction and two pairs of students (weaker students are paired with stronger ones) are trained to be assessors of one particular transaction by being helped to identify useful criteria that can be used in assessment by hearing example from the tape. Since there are two pairs that have been trained to assess the same transaction one half of the class can assess the other half and they can then change over. One student is assessed at a time. One assessor takes part in the transaction while his colleague concentrates on making an assessment.

	Takes part A	Makes assessment
Assessors	A	

	Takes part A
Student being assessed	B

Takes part B

The assessors do not need to be specific. If they feel that more work needs to be done they just mark it on the card of the student being assessed. At the end of the session every student should have been assessed on every one of his cue cards.

In a follow-up session those students who still need to do more work in some areas can work with those of their colleagues who have obtained mastery in those areas, using the model tape as an aid.

Conclusion

This model is cost effective if one wants to assess oral performance over a wide range of functions and then follow it up with individualized remedial work. The students enjoyed the bustle and activity. The reliability depends upon previous training and the ability of the students.

(e) Personal interviews

Aim

To evaluate students' ability to ask about and give personal factual information and to discuss the evaluation in a class group. Also to bring in an element of communicative doubt and elicit more spontaneous expression in which students can express their personalities more than in the other activities mentioned.

Activity

Four students from one class go into another class having prepared themselves to answer questions about themselves in topic areas such as job, hobbies, opinions and future plans. Some of the students are trained to do the assessment and others prepare questions to ask. The four students are interviewed one by one. No question can be asked to the same student twice and the teacher sees that two questions are asked by each student. The teacher also makes an assessment to check against the ones made by the students of those who asked the questions and those who have the information. The class then discusses the reason for any divergence in the assessments with a view to gaining a clearer view of the criteria involved.

Conclusion

The interview is the most 'realistic' of the models and is therefore less reliable as not everyone asks the same question and some questions are easier than others because the students can choose. There can be embarrassing pauses sometimes and the teacher needs to help out in such cases.

In all the models the teacher faces the problem of having to explain metalanguage eg categories of functions such as offers or suggestions, as well as the language to be learnt eg "Would you like an apple?", because the prompts in the cue cards use metalanguage. The teacher also has to give the students instructions and advice in English. If one had a single nationality group it would probably be easier to explain these things in the mother tongue initially.

SELECTIVE BIBLIOGRAPHY

Works credited

Chaix, P, and C O'Neill (1978) *Etude critique des modalités d'apprentissage autonome (autodidaxie et semi-autonomie) dans le domaine de l'acquisition des langues vivantes secondes. Rapport de synthèse.* Document: UNESCO ED-78/WS/58.

Dalin, A (1975) *Towards self-management of learning processes?* CCC/EES 75 9. Council of Europe, Strasbourg.

Developments in adult education structures, five national studies CCC/EES (76) 28. Council of Europe, Strasbourg.

Dickinson, L (1978) 'Autonomy, self-directed learning and individualization' in *Self-directed learning and autonomy, Cambridge 13–15 December 1976* Department of Linguistics, University of Cambridge.

Dieuzeide, H (1971) 'Technologie éducative II: l'école de demain' *L'éducation*, No. 91.

Dominicé, P (1973) *Continuing education for adults in the context of permanent education* CCC/EES (73) 35. Council of Europe, Strasbourg.

Henner-Stanchina, C (1976) *Autonomy: a viable strategy for adult language learners* Mémoire de maîtrise, Université de Nancy II.

Henner-Stanchina, C, and H Holec (1977) 'Evaluation in an autonomous learning scheme' in *Mélanges Pédagogiques 1977* CRAPEL, Nancy.

Illich, Y (1970) *Deschooling society*, Harper & Row, New York.

Illich, Y, *et al* (1973) *After deschooling, What?*, Harper & Row, New York.

Janne, H, (1977) *Organization, content and methods of adult education. Report* CCC/EES (77) 3. Council of Europe, Strasbourg.

Logan, G E (1970) 'Curricula for individualized instruction' in Lange, D L (*ed*) *Britannica Review of Foreign Language Education* Vol II.

Marbeau, M V (1977) *Autonomous work by pupils* CCC/EGT (77) 15 Council of Europe, Strasbourg.

Oskarsson, M (1980) *Approaches to self-assessment in foreign language learning* Pergamon, Oxford.

Porcher, L (1979) The functions of evaluation in a European unit/credit system for modern language learning by adults in the *Report of the Ludwigshafen-am-Rhein Symposium, 7–14 September 1977, on 'A European unit/credit system for modern language learning by adults'* CCC Council of Europe, Strasbourg.

Richterich, R, and J-L Chancerel (1980) *Identifying the needs of adults learning a foreign language* Pergamon, Oxford.

Scheffknecht, J J (1975) *The tutor* CCC, Council of Europe, Strasbourg.

Schwartz, B (1977) *Permanent education. Final report* CCC/EP (77) 8 revised. Council of Europe, Strasbourg.

Schwartz, B (1973) *L'éducation demain. Une étude de la fondation européene de la culture* Aubier Montaigne, Paris.

Sicre, M (1978) *Une expérience d'auto-enseignement de groupe en anglais (Public de IIIème âge)* Mémoire de maîtrise Université de Nancy II.

Trends towards self-management of adult education, six case studies (1976) CCC/EES (76) 29. Council of Europe, Strasbourg.

Trim, J L M (1980) 'Some possibilities and limitations of learning autonomy', in *Self-directed learning and autonomy, Cambridge 13–15 December 1976*. Department of Linguistics, University of Cambridge.

Trim, J L M (1980) *Developing a unit/credit scheme of adult language learning* Pergamon, Oxford.

Other works

Abe, D, C Henner-Stanchina and P Smith (1975) 'New approaches to autonomy: two experiments in self-directed learning' in *Mélanges Pédagogiques 1975* CRAPEL, Nancy.

Altman, H B (1977) 'Individualized foreign language instruction and systems thinking: symbiosis and synergism' *System*, 5, 2.

Altman, H B and C V James (*eds*) (1980) *Foreign language teaching: meeting individual needs* Pergamon, Oxford.

Cembalo, M, and M J Gremmo (1973) 'Autonomie de l'apprentissage: réalités et perspectives' in *Mélanges Pédagogiques 1973* CRAPEL, Nancy.

Cembalo, M, and H Holec (1973) 'Les langues aux adultes: pour une pédagogie de l'autonomie' in *Mélanges Pédagogiques 1973* CRAPEL, Nancy.

Curran, C A (1972) *Counselling-learning: a whole person approach to education* Grune & Stratton, New York.

Holec, H (1980) 'Learner training: meeting needs in self-directed learning' in Altman and James (*eds*) *Foreign language teaching: meeting individual needs* Pergamon, Oxford.

Mean, K (1976) 'Who needs a teacher? An alternative to the 'conversation' class' *Kielikeskusuutisia* 4, Language Centre for Finnish Universities, Jyväskylä.

Nieman, L L, and W F Smith (1977) 'Individualized instruction of foreign languages: a selected bibliography' *System*, 5, 2.

Papalia, A (1976) *Learner-centred language teaching methods and materials* Newbury House, Rowley, Mass.

Stevick, E (1973) 'Counselling learning: a whole person model for education' *Language Learning*, 23.

Towards independence in learning. Selected papers (1975) Group for Research and Innovation in Higher Education, Nuffield Foundation.

51

NOTES